OUR SISTER, PHOEBE
A SURVEY OF BIBLICAL AND
HISTORICAL SUPPORT FOR THE
DEACONESS IN THE MODERN
CHURCH

Rev. Jason Biette

OUR SISTER, PHOEBE
A SURVEY OF BIBLICAL AND
HISTORICAL SUPPORT FOR THE
DEACONESS IN THE MODERN
CHURCH

Printed in the United States of America

Scripture quotations are from The Holy Bible, English Standard
Version® (ESV®), copyright © 2001 by Crossway, a publishing
ministry of Good News Publishers. Used by permission. All
rights reserved.

First Printing, 2013

ISBN-13: 978-0615933764

ISBN-10: 0615933769

Oakwood Covenant Press
260 Oakwood Avenue
Troy, NY 12182

TABLE OF CONTENTS

Thesis

The Bible holds a high view of women and through the testimony of the Word and the testimony of the Church throughout history there is strong biblical support and historical evidence for women to be called to ministry within the church in the position of a properly and biblically defined role of deaconess.

Introduction

The debate of what role women can and should be allowed to play in the Church today continues to wage on, not only within evangelicalism, but also throughout the whole of Christendom. In fact, in writing on this topic in modern times, albeit from the perspective of the Roman Catholic Church, Zagano draws attention not only to the modern debate, but also to the rich history within the ancient Church when she writes: "significant scholarly evaluation of historical evidence, however, combined with worldwide calls for the restoration of the tradition of women deacons, drives contemporary discussion relative to the formalization of ministry by women through ordination to the diaconate."[1] The point of Zagano's research is to study the ancient ordination rites of the deaconess and the deacon in order to understand how the practices of the ancient Church can inform the modern Church. This is informative even for our study, as it clarifies not only that this is a topic which, in at least one sense, has been around for quite some time, but also is a topic

---

[1] Phyllis Zagano, "Remembering Tradition: Women's Monastic Rituals and the Diaconate." *Theological Studies* 72, no. 4 (2011): 788. (http://web.ebscohost.com.ezproxy.liberty.edu:2048/ehost/pdf viewer/pdfviewer?sid=1df7c8e1-5f01-4b34-88b3-53ab31b8a13c%40sessionmgr112&vid=4&hid=123, accessed May 5, 2013).

which continues to raise questions in the Church today.

     The purpose of the present study is to briefly survey the biblical and historical arguments for the role of the deaconess, showing that the best understanding of what ministry position women can and should hold within the church is ultimately found in properly defining the priesthood.

Defining the Terms

In order to study this topic, we must first strive to understand what should be considered as the two sides of the debate. Within this debate today, generally scholars and theologians fall in one of two camps; they are either egalitarians, or complementarians. Piper and Grudem define the egalitarian view when they write

> ... an avalanche of feminist literature has argued that there need be no difference between men's and women's roles – indeed, that to support gender-based role differences

is unjust discrimination. Within evangelical Christianity, the counterpart to this movement has been the increasing tendency to oppose any unique leadership role for men in the family and in the church. "Manhood" and "womanhood" as such are now often seen as irrelevant factors in determining fitness for leadership.[2]

The other side of the debate is represented by

the complementarians, and is ably defined by

Belleville when she writes that

the issue that divides traditionalists (now self-identified as "complementarians") and egalitarians today is not that of women in ministry per se (i.e., women exercising their spiritual gifts). It is rather *women in leadership*, for while a consensus has emerged regarding women and spiritual gifting, a great divide has emerged on the issue of women in

---

[2] John Piper and Wayne Grudem, "Preface," in *Recovering Biblical Manhood and Womanhood: A Response to Evangelical Feminism*, ed. John Piper and Wayne Grudem (Wheaton: Crossway Books, 1991), xiii.

leadership – especially women leading men.[3]

Belleville's definition of complementarianism, although from an egalitarian perspective, leads to the third and most important definition for this study. She correctly points out that in the modern Church this debate has more to do with leadership within the church than anything else, especially in terms of ministry. No one in the Church today seems to be denying the true calling of women to exercise their gifts in ministry to the body of Christ. Therefore, the attempt of this paper will be to define the debate in terms of the leadership in the church. For example, the main point of the debate should be in clearly defining, according to the Bible, what women *ought* to

---

[3] Linda L. Belleville, "Women in Ministry: An Egalitarian Perspective," in *Two Views on Women in Minsitry*, ed. James R. Beck (Grand Rapids: Zondervan, 2005), 23.

do. Egalitarians tend to rightly see that there are specific things that women can do in the Bible, and then extrapolate this out to the inclusion of everything. Therefore, they argue for women to be in leadership positions such as ministry of the Word within the church. Meanwhile, complementarians rightly recognize that, according to the Bible, women cannot function in pastoral roles. Therefore, they will extrapolate this out to many other roles within the church. Rev. Jim Jordan speaks directly to the issue when he explains the "kernel of the priestly office that men have, and that women do not."[4] Jordan

---

[4] James B. Jordan. *The Sociology of the Church: Essays in Reconstruction*, (Eugene: Wipf and Stock, 1999), 46.

goes on to show that the priest in the Old Testament, first represented by Adam, fulfilled by Jesus in the New Testament, and embodied by the Pastor in the Church was called to be a guard, specifically to guard the bride.[5] Rev. Jordan explains further. He writes

> Both men and women may perform the task of prophecy in both the general and special areas. Women may be teachers. Both men and women may perform the task of ruling in both the general and special areas. Women may be magistrates. Both men and women may perform the task of guarding in the general area, but only men may perform the task of guarding in the special area. Women may not be elders.[6]

---

[5] Ibid., 46.

[6] Ibid., 48

Jordan, who could be defined as a

Presbyterian, would define elder in the sense of pastor

or Minister of the Word.

This is the same argument which was once

taken up by C.S. Lewis when he wrote that "only one

wearing the masculine uniform can (provisionally, and

till the Parousia) represent the Lord to the Church:

for we are all, corporately and individually, feminine

to Him."[7]

This bears further emphasis. All involved in

the debate today, whether egalitarians or

complementarians tend to disregard the view of the

Church in the feminine role that God has placed her.

A very important and missing element to this debate

is in viewing the Church as Christ's Bride, and when

---

[7] C. S. Lewis, "Priestesses in the Church?" in *God in the Dock: Essays on Theology and Ethics* (Grand Rapids: Wm. B. Eerdmans, 1970), 239.

this is recovered it will help move the conversation along. Rev. Jeff Meyers, in writing about this very topic, states that

> Otherwise stated, the minister has an instrumental, ritual-symbolic function in the church service. He represents the Husband to the Bride. He acts for Jesus. He speaks for Jesus. He is authorized to act and speak. And everybody should know it. This is key. The minister is set apart to function in this capacity for the congregation.[8]

Rev. Meyers then goes on to conclude that this is why, within the Church, the person who leads worship, i.e. the Pastor, needs to be a man.[9] He writes

> By virtue of his office, he must represent the Husband to the Bride.

---

[8] Jeffrey J. Meyers. *The Lord's Service: The Grace of Covenant Renewal Worship*, (Moscow: Canon Press, 2003), 270.

[9] Ibid., 271.

A woman cannot do so. It would upset the entire fabric of God-ordained role relationships within the Church and home. The symbolism of male headship must be maintained in the corporate liturgy of the Church. The Church submits to her Lord as she receives from Him the Word and Sacraments by the mouth and the hands of the Pastor.[10]

Therefore, this paper posits that the best understanding of these things is in defining what it means to be a priest in the Bible, not in defining what women and men can do, nor in defining what role they can or can't play.

---

[10] Ibid., 271-272.

The Old Testament

The first thing that must be understood from the Old Testament is what, in God's economy, the priest was, who he represented, and what his work or duty was before God. For example, Erickson, in commenting on Hodge's understanding of atonement, writes that "the priest in the old dispensation interceded for all those for whom he offered sacrifice."[11] Erickson's definition, being

---

[11] Millard J. Erickson, *Christian Theology*, 2nd ed. (Grand Rapids: Baker Academic, 1998), 844.

limited to the context of the discussion on atonement, offers little insight. Grudem expands on this in his discussion of the offices of Christ, where he describes the Old Testament priesthood as a position which was chosen by God and included the duties of sacrifice, praise and prayer.[12] He concludes that "they "sanctified" the people or made them acceptable to come into God's presence, albeit in a limited way during the Old Testament period."[13] Although Grudem offers a little more detail in his definition of the Old Testament priest, this paper would submit that there is still something missing, and it is a more full understanding of the Old Testament office of

---

[12] Wayne Grudem, *Systematic Theology: An Introduction to Biblical Doctrine*, (Grand Rapids: Zondervan, 1994), 626.

[13] Ibid.

priest, which speaks to the debate regarding women in the Church today.

Rev. James B. Jordan gives a much fuller biblical treatment of this topic than what would normally be found in a typical systematic theology. Jordan explains why the typical answers are inadequate. First, he appeals to the role of the priest representing the people and shows that if the priest's role were merely representation then there would be no reason to disqualify women from the office, because women would be the best representatives of the Bride.[14] Second, he appeals to the priest representing God and shows that this is inadequate because throughout the Bible women represented

---

[14] James B. Jordan, *The Sociology of the Church: Essays in Reconstruction*, (Eugene: Wipf and Stock Publishers, 1999), 46.

their husbands and rulers.[15] Through the elimination

of these two arguments of what makes the priesthood

special, Jordan then concludes

> The correct answer is this: The priest
> is a guard, and as a guard, he must
> guard something. What he guards is
> the Bride, and as the guardian of the
> Bride, he must be a figure (symbol) of
> the Father/Husband/Son. That is, he
> must be a male.[16]

After drawing this conclusion Jordan then

explains his point from Genesis chapters 2 and 3.

Jordan begins by defining the two tasks that God

gives to Adam in the garden; which he defines as

kingly and priestly. Jordan then describes the priestly

task in terms of guarding the garden.[17] Jordan then

further defines this priestly task in terms of food, or

---

[15] Ibid.

[16] Ibid.

[17] Ibid.

more specifically guarding the "sacramental eating."[18]

He continues when he writes that

> Man failed the priestly task. He stood by and permitted his wife to interact with the serpent. He failed to guard her, or the garden. He permitted her to partake of the table of demons. He received instruction from her mouth, and food from her hand, the reverse of the proper order. Now, the important thing to note at this point is that the woman was not present when the man entered into the kingly task. She was brought in to help him with it, making her a queen. But, when the test regarding the priestly task came about, it was precisely in terms of whether or not the man would guard his wife.[19]

There are several conclusions that can and should be drawn from the points that Jordan makes. First, this understanding of the priestly task is what informs the priesthood throughout the whole of the

---

[18] Ibid., 47.

[19] Ibid.

Bible to follow. Priests are judged based on whether they stay true to their task of guarding (Lev. 10), and Apostles are given the keys by Jesus (Mt. 16:19-20). Second, although this clearly defines why women can't be priests (or Pastors for that matter), it leaves available to them far more ministries within the Church than it closes off. Regarding the specific question of deacons Jordan writes

> How about women as deacons? Impossible, because to be a deacon you have to be a man. How about deaconesses, then? No problem. Both in the Old and in the New Testament, certain women are set aside to assist the elders with certain tasks (Ex. 38:8; 1Sam. 2:22; Jud. 11:40; Matt. 27:55-56; Luke 8:2-3; Rom. 16:1; Phil. 4:2-3; 1 Tim. 3:11; 1 Tim. 5:3-10). This, of course, is not a special ruling function.[20]

---

[20] Ibid., 48-49.

The New Testament

In regards to this discussion, there seems to be much more scholarly work in New Testament studies available, which as stated earlier, is at least on some level because very little has yet been done in defining the conversation in terms of the role of the priest in the Bible. Therefore, recognizing that it is in the New Testament where one generally finds the institution of the diaconate and the role of women not only in the life of Christ, but also in the life of the early Church, scholars spend the majority of their work here. An able example of this can be found in Reymond's systematic theology where he writes that "deacons, first chosen to assist the apostles (Acts 6:1-7), where thereafter appointed to assist the elders."[21]

Much of New Testament scholarly work revolves around Romans 16:1, which states in the English Standard Version, "I commend to you our sister Phoebe, a servant of the church at Cenchreae." Scholars focus on the Greek word of servant (*diakonon*), the same word which is translated as deacon in other New Testament passages. Even the translators of the English Standard Version offer a footnote for the word servant and d*eaconess* as another possible translation of the word.

---

[21]Robert L. Reymond, *A New Systematic Theology of the Christian Faith*, 2nd ed. (Nashville: Thomas Nelson Inc., 1998), 899.

Various commentators and scholars all hold different opinions regarding this verse and Paul's use of *diakonon*. Murray, in his commentary on Romans writes that

> It is common to give Phoebe the title of "deaconess" and regard her as having performed an office in the church corresponding to that which belonged to men who exercised the office of deacon (*cf.* Phil. 1:1; I Tim. 3L8-13). Though the word for "servant" is the same as is used for deacon in the instances cited, yet the word is also used to denote the person performing any type of ministry. If Phoebe ministered to the saints, as is evident from verse 2, then she would be a servant of the church and there is neither need nor warrant to suppose that she occupied or exercised what amounted to an ecclesiastical office comparable to that of the diaconate.[22]

---

[22] John Murray, *The Epistle to the Romans: The English Text with Introduction, Exposition and Notes*, (Grand Rapids: Wm. B. Eerdmans, 1997), 226.

In fact, Murray goes on to explain that there is
nothing in the passage that specifically speaks to those
duties which are considered especially set aside for
deacons, and sees no strong reason to view this as a
special office that Phoebe held in the church.[23]

On the other hand, Calvin, although never
referring to Phoebe as a deaconess, does refer to her
as an "assistant," and in several locations refers to the
office which she holds.[24] In fact, in his most
definitive statement on this verse he writes that

> … this service, of which he speaks as
> to what it was, he teaches us in
> another place, in 1 Tim. v. 9, for as the
> poor were supported from the public
> treasury of the Church, so they were
> taken care of by those in public
> offices, and for this charge widows

---

[23] Ibid.

[24] John Calvin, *Commentaries on the Epistle of Paul the Apostle to the Romans*, trans. John Owen (Grand Rapids: Baker Book House, 2005), 542.

were chosen, who being free from domestic concerns, and cumbered by no children, wished to consecrate themselves wholly to God by religious duties, they were therefore received into this office as those who had wholly given up themselves, and became bound to their charge in a manner like him, who having hired out his own labours, ceases to be free and to be his own master.[25]

Another example is Barth, who seems to not see the need for much comment at all about Phoebe, either having no interest in the controversy, or more likely for Barth, having his interest found in other areas. He, very simply and offhandedly writes that "in the middle of the first century a community-sister took the letter from Corinth to Rome."[26]

---

[25] Ibid., 543.

[26] Karl Barth. *The Epistle to the Romans*, trans. Edwyn C. Hoskyns (Oxford: Oxford University Press, 1968), 536.

The most interesting modern commentary may be that of Schreiner, who spends a considerable amount of space defending the view that Phoebe was a deacon in the early church. He begins the section by writing that "she is a "deacon" of the church in Cenchreae."[27] Schreiner then describes the debate regarding Phoebe's position, recognizing that there are strong arguments against seeing her in an official capacity, especially when the word is understood as a description of various forms of service within the church.[28] Ultimately he concludes that Phoebe held the office of deacon, and he very ably lays out three arguments

> First, 1 Tim. 3:11 probably identifies women as deacons. Second, the

---

[27] Thomas R. Schreiner. *Romans*, (Grand Rapids: Baker Books, 1998), 786.

[28] Ibid., 787.

designation "deacon of the church in Cenchreae" suggests that Phoebe served in this special capacity, for this is the only occasion in which the term [*diakonos*] is linked with a particular local church. Third, the use of the masculine noun [*diakonos*] also suggests that the office is intended.[29]

Schreiner does caution against reading the modern, more developed view of the diaconate into this very early occasion and position, while at the same time acknowledging that the early church would have very quickly realized a need for women to serve in such capacities in order to help with difficult and sensitive issues which would arise with an influx of new members of the church from both sexes.[30]

---

[29] Ibid.

[30] Ibid.

Church History

The last area of this survey is in the realm of Church history, and recognizing that the practices of the Church throughout her history do bear testimony on the practices of the Church today.

For example, Zagano's research has already been referred to, but her studies in the ancient practices of the church, especially in ordaining women to the position of deacon, warrants a closer look. She writes that "ordination ceremonies for women deacons are known from the early third century. They preserve early literary and epigraphical evidence of women deacons in many regions, often against pressure to end the practice of ordination of women as deacons."[31] Although her research is not limited to the information above, it begins to lay the groundwork for viewing what we will ultimately refer to as deaconesses as a longstanding practice within the Church.

Latourette has a much more extensive study of the deaconess in the church, corroborating and adding to that which was found by Zagano beginning in the second century. He begins by explaining that this was the century when a sharp distinction was

---

[31] Phyllis Zagano, "Remembering Tradition: Women's Monastic Rituals and the Diaconate." *Theological Studies* 72, no. 4 (2011): 788-789. (http://web.ebscohost.com.ezproxy.liberty.edu:2048/ehost/pdf viewer/pdfviewer?sid=1df7c8e1-5f01-4b34-88b3-53ab31b8a13c%40sessionmgr112&vid=4&hid=123, accessed May 5, 2013).

beginning to be made between those who were ordained as clergy, and all others representing the laity.[32] This distinction, as posited by Latourette, is partly what brought about the position of deaconess, where he writes that "deaconesses were to be found in the eastern part of the Empire, with the responsibility of caring for the members of their sex."[33] Jumping some 1700 years ahead he points out that "in 1849 Konrad Wilhelm Loehe (1808-1872), a pastor in Neuendettelsau in Bavaria, founded a Lutheran society for the Inner Mission and four years later he inaugurated a union of deaconesses."[34] It

---

[32] Kenneth Scott Latourette, *A History of Christianity: Beginnings to 1500*, (Peabody: Prince Press, 1997), 133.

[33] Ibid.

[34] Kenneth Scott Latourette, *A History of Christianity: Reformation to the Present*, (Peabody: Prince Press, 1997), 1136.

seems that this was the beginning of a very important

ministerial movement within Germany. Latourette

notes

> In 1833 Theodore Fliedner, a pastor at
> Kaiserswerth, a destitute parish, began
> the use of deaconesses to assist him.
> He founded a training school for
> them. They nursed the sick as well as
> cared for the spiritually destitute.
> Partly stimulated by this precedent, in
> 1894, in Germany nearly eight
> thousand deaconesses were serving in
> hospitals, poor-houses, orphanages,
> and schools, and as parish-helpers.[35]

Finally, Latourette chronicles the rise of

deaconesses in Sweden, the establishment of a school

for training in England (much like the

aforementioned school in Germany), and the rise of

deaconesses in English Methodism.[36]

---

[35] Ibid.

[36] Ibid., 1147, 1167, 1183.

It should be noted that this study does not posit that the practices of the Church throughout her history should be viewed as prescriptive for determining doctrine, or even in this case, the correct ecclesiology that the Church should be following. It may even be too strong to state that what the Church does in the past should set a precedent for what the Church should do in the present and in the future. There is always a place for critiquing and correcting errors of the past. At the same time, it is also important to note that as the Church established the role of deaconess as early as the second century, and continued, in some circles, to maintain and expand that role through the Reformation and even into the modern era, it is expressive of how the Church (especially the early Church) interpreted and applied everything from the Scriptures which has already been discussed. Furthermore, this paper would submit that the example from Germany in the 1800's may speak to the modern evangelical church's anemic state in terms of true biblical social justice and ministry. Very often the critique is that the modern church has given up these ministries to the para-church movement, or worse, to the government. It may be the case that the conservative evangelical movement, in a right response to creeping liberalism and feminism in the Church, went too far by overreacting and putting some of the church's best workers, the women, in a position of not being able to work according to what God's Word would have them do.

Conclusion

Those who are labeled as conservative, or label themselves as conservative, in the Church today, do find that they generally, in their understanding of God's Word and its application to the life of the Church, are at odds with most of the rest of the culture around them. Strauch recognizes this when he writes that

> there is much about biblical eldership that offends church-going people today: the concept of elders who provide pastoral care, a plurality of pastors, and the idea of so-called "lay"

> or nonclerical pastor elders. Yet
> nothing is more objectionable in the
> minds of contemporary people than
> the biblical concept of an all-male
> eldership. A biblical eldership,
> however, must be an all-male
> eldership.[37]

In the controversial age that the Church finds itself in,
his point is well taken. Yet, he later writes that "we
need to be perfectly clear about the biblical teaching
regarding women and men as fully equal in
personhood, dignity, and value, but distinct in their
gender roles."[38] Again, we would agree with Strauch's
assessment, while at the same time recognizing that
his stance creates a tension which drives the
egalitarian to make accusations of double-speak. This

---

[37] Alexander Strauch, *Biblical Eldership: An Urgent Call to Restore Biblical Church Leadership*, 3rd ed. (Littleton: Lewis and Roth Publishers, 1995), 51.

[38] Ibid.

paper submits that that tension created can be alleviated in the position of deaconess.

This leads to another objection which could be leveled by egalitarians. Why create the position of deaconess when the Church could just ordain female deacons? This has as much to do with modern ecclesiology as any other topic addressed by this paper. Maintaining the position of deaconess allows for there to be continued distinction with regards to the guarding aspect of the pastorate which we maintain women cannot rightly do. This recognizes varying ecclesiologies within Protestant Christianity. As Coppes writes, "The three-office position sees three ordinary offices in the New Testament: teaching elder, ruling elder, and deacon."[39] This is

---

[39] Leonard J. Coppes, "Three New Testament Offices," in *Order in the Offices: Essays Defining the Roles of*

straightforward enough, and generally speaking, within Presbyterianism there would be no problem. Yet when we get to those churches which follow more of an episcopal form of government there is quite a discrepancy in how the position of deacon is viewed. Here the office of deacon in an ordained position, which is the first step to the priesthood. In the Common Prayer Book is states that

> It is evident unto all men, diligently reading Holy Scripture and ancient Authors, that from the Apostles' time there have been these Orders of Ministers in Christ's Church, - Bishops, Priests, and Deacons. Which offices were evermore had in such reverend estimation, that no man might presume to execute any of them, except he were first called, tried, examined, and known to have such

---

Church Officers, ed. Mark R. Brown (Duncansville: Classic Presbyterian Government Resources, 1993), 203.

qualities as are requisite for the same...[40]

In reiterating the episcopal view of the diaconate as part of the priesthood, further instructions explain that the person ordained a deacon must, under normal circumstances, remain in that office for one year before being able to then enter into the priesthood.[41] Therefore, understanding women fulfilling a separate role of deaconess takes into account most forms of ecclesiology in the modern Church.

Finally, there is no intention to offer the definitive word on this subject in this paper. The Church, even modern scholarship, continues to

---

[40] Protestant Episcopal Church, *The Book of Common Prayer and Administration of the Sacraments and Other Rites and Ceremonies of the Church*, (New York: The Church Pension Fund, 1945), 529.

[41] Ibid., 535.

produce exegesis and strong arguments on both sides. For example, Agan writes that "while no one of these arguments is definitive, the cumulative evidence points toward Phoebe's being neither a "deacon" nor a "servant," but what we today might call a "representative.""[42] While at the same time Perry concludes that

> though Paul does not define the role of "the deacons" specifically, he shows that they are proven men and women (1 Tim. 3:8-13), who serve as "agents" or "representatives" of their local assembly through their own "ministries," "gifts," and "activities" (1 Cor. 12:4-6), and in specific tasks that the congregation authorizes (Rom. 16:1-2; cf. Acts 6:1-6).[43]

---

[42] Clarence DeWitt Agan III, "Deacons, Deaconesses, and Denominational Discussions: Romans 16:1 as a Test Case." *Presbyterion* 34, no. 2 (Fall 2008): 108. (http://web.ebscohost.com.ezproxy.liberty.edu:2048/ehost/pdf viewer/pdfviewer?sid=1df7c8e1-5f01-4b34-88b3-53ab31b8a13c%40sessionmgr112&vid=16&hid=123, accessed May 5, 2013).

[43] Gregory R. Perry, "Phoebe of Cenchreae and "Women" of Ephesus: "Deacons" in the Earliest Church."

Ultimately a balanced approach is what will

prove to be the best approach regarding this topic.

As Yarbrough points out that "women's own

distinctive callings and gifts, which include didactic

and leadership skills, should be maximized, not

marginalized."[44] This paper heartily agrees with

Yarbrough's point, positing through our

understanding of the role of the priest in the Old

Testament, through Paul's referencing Phoebe as a

deaconess in the New Testament Church, and

Presbyterion 36, no. 1 (Spring 2010): 36.
(http://web.ebscohost.com.ezproxy.liberty.edu:2048/ehost/pdf
viewer/pdfviewer?sid=1df7c8e1-5f01-4b34-88b3-
53ab31b8a13c%40sessionmgr112&vid=21&hid=123,
accessed May 5, 2013).

[44] Robert W. Yarbrough, "Women and Ministry:
Fidelity to Scripture in the Unity of Faith." *Presbyterion* 35,
no. 2 (Fall 2009): 65.
(http://web.ebscohost.com.ezproxy.liberty.edu:2048/ehost/pdf
viewer/pdfviewer?sid=1df7c8e1-5f01-4b34-88b3-
53ab31b8a13c%40sessionmgr112&vid=24&hid=123 accessed
May 5, 2013).

through the testimony of the Church for most of her

history that the position of deaconess in the Church

allows for women to best utilize their distinct gifts in

a ministerial capacity while allowing for the balance in

the unique role that men are called to play as the

guardians of the Bride.

.

Bibliography

Agan III, Clarence DeWitt. "Deacons, Deaconesses, and
        Denominational Discussions: Romans 16:1 as a Test
        Case." *Presbyterion* 34, no. 2 (Fall 2008): 93-108.
        (http://web.ebscohost.com.ezproxy.liberty.edu:2048/e
        host/pdfviewer/pdfviewer?sid=1df7c8e1-5f01-4b34-
        88b3-
        53ab31b8a13c%40sessionmgr112&vid=16&hid=123
        accessed May 5, 2013).

Barth, Karl. *The Epistle to the Romans.* Translated by Edwyn C.
        Hoskyns. Oxford: Oxford University Press, 1968.

Belleville, Lind L. "Women in Ministry: An Egalitarian
        Perspective," in *Two Views on Women in Minsitry*, edited
        by James R. Beck, 21-103. Grand Rapids: Zondervan,
        2005.

Calvin, John. *Commentaries on the Epistle of Paul the Apostle to the
        Romans.* Translated by John Owen. Grand Rapids:
        Baker Book House, 2005.

Coppes, Leonard J. "Three New Testament Offices," in *Order in
        the Offices: Essays Defining the Roles of Church Officers.*

Edited by Mark R. Brown, 203-216. Duncansville: Classic Presbyterian Government Resources, 1993.

Erickson, Millard J. *Christian Theology*. 2nd ed. Grand Rapids: Baker Academic, 1998.

Grudem, Wayne. *Systematic Theology: An Introduction to Biblical Doctrine*. Grand Rapids: Zondervan, 1994.

Jordan, James B. *The Sociology of the Church: Essays in Reconstruction*. Eugene: Wipf and Stock, 1999.

Latourette, Kenneth Scott. *A History of Christianity: Beginnings to 1500*. Peabody: Prince Press, 1997.

————. *A History of Christianity: Reformation to the Present*. Peabody: Prince Press, 1997.

Lewis, C. S. "Priestesses in the Church?" in *God in the Dock: Essays on Theology and Ethics*, 238-239. Grand Rapids: Wm. B. Eerdmans, 1970.

Meyers, Jeffrey J. *The Lord's Service: The Grace of Covenant Renewal Worship*. Moscow: Canon Press, 2003.

Murray, John. *The Epistle to the Romans: The English Text with Introduction, Exposition and Notes*. Grand Rapids: Wm. B. Eerdmans, 1997.

Perry, Gregory R. "Phoebe of Cenchreae and "Women" of Ephesus: "Deacons" in the Earliest Church." *Presbyterion* 36, no. 1 (Spring 2010): 9-36. (http://web.ebscohost.com.ezproxy.liberty.edu:2048/ehost/pdfviewer/pdfviewer?sid=1df7c8e1-5f01-4b34-88b3-53ab31b8a13c%40sessionmgr112&vid=21&hid=123, accessed May 5, 2013).

Piper, John and Wayne Grudem. "Preface," in *Recovering Biblical Manhood and Womanhood: A Response to Evangelical*

Feminism, edited by John Piper and Wayne Grudem, xiii-xv. Wheaton: Crossway Books, 1991.

Protestant Episcopal Church. *The Book of Common Prayer and Administration of the Sacraments and Other Rites and Ceremonies of the Church*. New York: The Church Pension Fund, 1945.

Reymond, Robert L. *A New Systematic Theology of the Christian Faith*. 2nd ed. Nashville: Thomas Nelson Inc., 1998.

Schreiner, Thomas R. *Romans*. Grand Rapids: Baker Books, 1998.

Strauch, Alexander. *Biblical Eldership: An Urgent Call to Restore Biblical Church Leadership*. 3rd ed. Littleton: Lewis and Roth Publishers, 1995.

Yarbrough, Robert W. "Women and Ministry: Fidelity to Scripture in the Unity of Faith." *Presbyterion* 35, no. 2 (Fall 2009): 65-81. (http://web.ebscohost.com.ezproxy.liberty.edu:2048/ehost/pdfviewer/pdfviewer?sid=1df7c8e1-5f01-4b34-88b3-53ab31b8a13c%40sessionmgr112&vid=24&hid=123, accessed May 5, 2013).

Zagano, Phyllis. "Remembering Tradition: Women's Monastic Rituals and the Diaconate." *Theological Studies* 72, no. 4 (2011): 787-811. (http://web.ebscohost.com.ezproxy.liberty.edu:2048/ehost/pdfviewer/pdfviewer?sid=1df7c8e1-5f01-4b34-88b3-53ab31b8a13c%40sessionmgr112&vid=4&hid=123, accessed May 5, 2013).